FAMOUS
LAST
WORDS

FAMOUS
LAST
WORDS

An Anthology

Edited by Claire Cock-Starkey

Bodleian Library
UNIVERSITY OF OXFORD

First published in 2016 by the Bodleian Library
Broad Street, Oxford OX1 3BG

www.bodleianshop.co.uk

ISBN: 978 1 85124 251 1

Introduction and selection © Claire Cock-Starkey, 2016

Designed by Dot Little at the Bodleian Library
Typeset by JCS Publishing Services Ltd in 12pt on 14.5pt
Adobe Garamond Pro
Printed and bound in Croatia by Zrinski D.D. on
80gsm Munken Premium Cream

British Library Catalogue in Publishing Data
A CIP record of this publication is available from the
British Library

Introduction

Mark Twain gave great consideration to the concept of preserving final words. He thought last words should 'enable him to say something smart with his latest gasp and launch him into eternity with grandeur'. But he also cautioned that 'a man is apt to be too much fagged and exhausted, both in body and mind, at such a time, to be reliable.' So he advised that last words should be pre-planned, written down, shown to friends and discussed.

Unfortunately, Twain did not take his own advice and in fact his final words to his daughter were frustratingly incomplete, perhaps proving the old adage of best-laid plans. Twain, lying on his deathbed, addressed his daughter Clara, saying, 'Goodbye.' He then took her hand and tantalizingly whispered, 'If we meet ...', before falling asleep and dying a few hours later.

We all wish to leave the world uttering something profound and yet that rarely happens because, sadly, death tends to get in the way. But this collection of final words offers some truly wonderful stories, historical insights, propaganda, aching sentiments and pithy bon mots. Each one ushers us back to a point in time, allowing us to float like spectres round the deathbed, each poignant utterance bringing a different version of the final moment.

If we are thinking about last words, then it is inevitable we are also thinking about death. In their introduction to *The Art of Dying* (1930), Francis Birrell and F.L. Lucas assert: 'There are indeed three possible ways of dying – in a coma, in delirium or semi-consciousness, and in full possession of the faculties.' Death, therefore, comes in many guises, and this is reflected in any collection of final words. Some meet death with a lucid mind, slowly drifting off with family gathered around, allowing the composition of a suitably sentimental final sentence. Others are much taken by surprise by a sudden death, or even murder, and their final words reflect this. Some poor souls leave this world in delirium and their parting words may be completely arbitrary or nonsensical.

In a long and drawn-out death there might be many times when the ailing person is expected to expire, only to rally and live out a few more days. One can almost picture a scene whereby loved ones are gathered round a deathbed, feverishly noting down every utterance, just in case it proves to be the final one. One cannot help but think that many of these famous last moments have been curated by those present; much as 'history is written by the victors', last words are written by the living. There is an urge to represent our loved and revered icons in the best possible light, therefore it is almost inevitable that many last words released to the public have perhaps been tinkered with.

On examination, some of the most famous last words are found to be apocryphal. This has not always prevented me from using them in this collection as they still provide insight into our perceptions of the character of the person who is supposed to have uttered them. Much can be inferred from the last words that have become famous – whether they were indeed last or not – such as the words attributed to Charles II, who was supposed to have entreated: 'Let not poor Nelly starve', referring to his mistress, the actress Nell Gwyn. It is interesting to note that it was this sentiment that proved enduring, despite his actual last words being: 'You must pardon me, gentlemen, for being a most unconscionable time a-dying.'

Why then do we seek to collect final words? We are often looking for a profound message or perhaps an anecdote that beautifully encapsulates the character of the person. In this case the collector wants to present the dying person in a good light, which in itself can lead to different accounts of what those last words were. In the official account of George V's last moments, Buckingham Palace released his final words as: 'How is the Empire?' – a sentence that reveals a monarch's deep care for his realm and his people. However, it later emerged from eyewitness accounts that George, on being reassured that he would soon be taken to Bognor for recuperation, actually uttered the rather less thoughtful: 'Bugger Bognor!'

If we could choose our moment to die, we might craft the most perfect final sentence to sum up our life's work or to pass on a vital message, but death is so very often not like this. The great chemist Louis Pasteur, who developed the technique now known as pasteurization, among many other discoveries, might perhaps have chosen to pass on some nugget of his genius in his last moments. Unfortunately, his actual last recorded words were the rather practical 'I cannot' in response to someone offering him a glass of milk – it is not recorded whether or not the milk was pasteurized.

Even if you had planned a great final sentence, death may well take you by surprise. Take the celebrated composer Richard Wagner, for example. He was suddenly struck down by a heart attack and as he fell, he dropped his watch. As he saw it fall, the last words to escape his mouth were: 'Oh, my watch …' A person's final words can reveal much about the circumstances in which they died. The final words of the writer Saki, who was picked off by a sniper during the First World War, were: 'Put that bloody cigarette out' – very evocative of the tragic circumstances of his death. Similarly for the British Prime Minister Spencer Perceval, who was assassinated in the lobby of the House of Commons, whose final utterance was the terrible realization of what had occurred: 'Oh my God.'

Those looking for a deeper meaning in the last words of a great person may be truly stumped by those of Henry David Thoreau. The great naturalist was suffering in delirium and his final, mumbled words appear to be entirely random: 'Moose … Indian …'

Many last words have been recorded with propaganda in mind. Those of a religious nature may have wanted their loved ones to ensure that the final speech released to the public reflected their religious beliefs. Leader of the Protestant Reformation, Martin Luther was asked on his deathbed if he stood by his teachings of the scripture, and his final word was an emphatic 'Yes!'

This goes both ways, and it seems that the final words of a number of atheists have been used against them to imply a conversion at the end or a fear of death. Indeed, a number of versions of final words have been conjured up for Voltaire, a famous critic of the dominant Catholic Church, including this apocryphal utterance, in which he appears to entirely change his tack: 'I am abandoned by God and man! I will give you half of what I am worth if you will give me six months' life. Then I shall go to hell; and you will go with me. O Christ! O Jesus Christ!' The more enduring accounts of Voltaire's final words preserve his wit and disdain, such as the version where he sees his bedside lamp flare and quips: 'What, the flames already?' Or the version I have used in this collection (which, although possibly apocryphal, appears to be the most accepted), in which, when asked to renounce Satan, Voltaire replied: 'Now, now, my good man, this is not time to be making enemies.'

The nature of a deathbed scene, whereby many loved ones gather round the bed to say farewell, has meant that there are often a number of people present at the moment of death, meaning that different interpretations of last words may be offered. This was the case with William Pitt the Younger, whose final words have been the subject of some dispute, with some saying he uttered, 'Oh my country, how I leave thee!' while others offer the rather more positive: 'Oh my country, how I love thee!'

Due to the cultural importance we have placed on a person's last words, quite frequently what are reported as the final words were clearly not the actual last words, but the last meaningful or most appropriate words spoken by that person. One example is the great wit Oscar Wilde, whose last words are given as the suitably amusing: 'My wallpaper and I are fighting a duel to the death. One or other of us has got to go.' However, considering that Wilde was dying from meningitis it seems likely that something rather more mundane may have been his actual last words.

Where death is sudden or unexpected, final words may not have been recorded as, at the time, no one realized they would be the subject's last words. In cases such as these a final letter is sometimes used as the source of the final words. These can often be most profound as the person might be aware when writing the letter that it was their last chance to pass on a message. This is most poignant in the letters written by those who committed suicide. The last letter of Virginia Woolf to her husband, before she filled her pockets with stones and drowned herself in the river Ouse, provides a very sad glimpse into her state of mind: 'I have a feeling I shall go mad. I cannot go on any longer in these terrible times. I hear voices and cannot concentrate on my work. I have fought against it but cannot fight any longer. I owe my happiness to you but cannot go on and spoil your life.'

The final entry in the journal of Robert Falcon Scott, written as he huddled dying in a tent in the Antarctic wilderness, knowing that his quest to be the first to reach the South Pole had been unsuccessful and that the survival of his comrades was hopeless, reveals something of his desperate state of mind: 'For God's sake look after our people.'

Another of that expedition, Captain Lawrence Oates, will be forever remembered for uttering the most selfless final words. Realizing that the severe frostbite he was suffering from was holding up the team as they battled through the snow and ice to reach base camp, Oates felt his only option was to sacrifice himself so that they might have a chance to survive. Walking from the tent to his doom, he uttered the now-immortal lines: 'I am just going outside, I may be some time.'

Some final words can give us a snapshot of a moment of history through a number of players. For example, two men present at the signing of the Declaration of Independence, former US presidents Thomas Jefferson and John Adams, coincidentally died on the same day, and even more coincidentally that same day was 4 July, exactly fifty years after the Declaration was signed. Jefferson, on his deathbed, was concerned with the date, his final words: 'Is it the fourth?' Adams remembered his friend and colleague in his last words: 'Thomas Jefferson still lives.' Except of course he was wrong, as Jefferson had died just hours before.

The same is true of the death of French Revolutionary leader Jean-Paul Marat, who was murdered in his bath by Girondist sympathizer Charlotte Corday. Marat suffered from a serious skin condition which meant he had to soak in a bath for hours at a time, thus when Corday asked to see him she was ushered into his bathroom-*cum*-study. Corday pretended to give the names of some Girondist traitors in order to gain admittance, and when Marat assured her they would be arrested, she took the knife concealed in her dress and stabbed him in the heart. Marat's final words were to his wife: 'Help me, my dear friend.' Corday was arrested and sentenced to death for the crime. Her final words reflect her fascination at seeing the newfangled guillotine up close for the first time: 'I have a right to be curious, I have never seen one before. It is the toilette of death, but it leads to immortality.'

Some of the most tragic final words were uttered by the ever-optimistic, those who seemed unprepared for death, believing they would yet recover. American actor Douglas Fairbanks' last words were the perhaps delusional: 'I've never felt better', and Mormon leader Brigham Young exclaimed: 'I feel better.' Occasionally, last words really do capture the essence of a person. Norwegian playwright Henrik Ibsen lived up to his reputation as a master of realism right to the very end. A nurse at his bedside commented that Ibsen seemed a little better and Ibsen replied: 'On the contrary.'

Sometimes there are a series of conversations which make up a person's last words and the more interesting bits are the ones that are chosen to be shared as 'official' last words. Lord Byron had a number of final speeches attributed to him, including: 'Poor Greece! I have given her my time, my means, my health – and now I give her my life! What could I do more?' and 'Shall I sue for mercy? Come, come, no weakness; let's be a man to the last.' But in an account of Byron's last hours by his companion Count Peter Gamba, Byron's actual final words were given as the rather more prosaic: 'I must sleep now.'

Our obsession with preserving the final words of notable people shows no sign of abating. Just recently, the final words of Apple co-founder Steve Jobs were released to the public. They are words that reflect his curious spirit and positive frame of mind when faced with death: 'Oh wow. Oh wow. Oh wow.'

And perhaps in the most modern rendering of final words, the beloved fantasy author Terry Pratchett, aware that death was fast approaching, composed a series of final tweets to be released by his family as he died. Echoing Pratchett's personification of Death from his Discworld stories in which the black-clothed figure rides a horse called Binky and always speaks in capital letters, Pratchett tweeted:

'AT LAST, SIR TERRY, WE MUST WALK TOGETHER.' This was followed by: 'Terry took Death's arm and followed him through the doors and on to the black desert under the endless night.' And then finally: 'The End.'

FAMOUS
LAST
WORDS

John Adams (1735–1826)

Second US President and Founding Father

'Thomas Jefferson still lives.'

Unfortunately Adams was wrong, as Jefferson had in fact died that very morning.

John Quincy Adams (1767–1848)

Sixth US President

'It is the last of earth! I am content!'

Joseph Addison (1672–1719)

English poet and essayist

'See in what peace a Christian can die!'

Prince Albert (1819–1861)

To his wife, Queen Victoria:

'Good little woman.'

Louisa May Alcott (1832–1888)

Author of Little Women

'Is it not meningitis?'

Thomas B. Aldrich (1836–1907)

American poet

'In spite of it all, I am going to sleep;
put out the lights.'

Alexander II of Russia (1818–1881)

Mortally wounded by a bomb thrown at his carriage:

'Home to the palace to die.'

Alexander the Great (356–323 BC)

*When asked who he would like to succeed him, he was
said to have replied:*

'The strongest.'

Ethan Allen (1739–1789)

American Revolutionary general. In response to a doctor who tried to comfort him by saying, 'The angels are waiting for you', Allen replied:

'Waiting are they? Waiting are they? Well, let 'em wait.'

John André (1750–1780)

A major in the British Army at the time of the American Revolution, executed as a spy

'It will be but a momentary pang.'

Anne of Austria (1601–1666)

Daughter of Philip III of Spain and mother of Louis XIV of France. Regarding her hands, which had once been much admired for their beauty:

'Observe how they are swelled; time to depart.'

Ludovico Ariosto (1479–1533)

Italian poet

'This is not my home.'

Jane Austen (1775–1817)

When asked if she required anything, she replied:

'I want nothing but death.'

Johann Sebastian Bach (1685–1750)

'Don't cry for me, for I go where music is born.'

Robert Baden-Powell (1857–1941)

Founder of the Boy Scouts. In a last letter addressed to 'Dear Scouts' found among his papers, he wrote:

'"Be Prepared" in this way, to live happy and to die happy – stick to your Scout promise always – even after you have ceased to be a boy – and God help you to do it.'

Walter Bagehot (1826–1877)

British journalist and essayist. He refused help rearranging his pillows, saying:

'Let me have my own fidgets.'

Jean Sylvain Bailly (1736–1793)

French astronomer and philosopher. Executed during the French Revolution – as he was paraded through the freezing streets a spectator called out: 'Bailly, you tremble.' Bailly replied:

'My friend, it is only from cold.'

P.T. Barnum (1810–1891)

American showman

'How were the receipts today at Madison Square Garden?'

J.M. Barrie (1860–1937)

British author

'I can't sleep.'

Clarence W. Barron (1855–1928)

American financial journalist

'What's the news?'

John Barrymore (1882–1942)

American actor

'Die? I should say not, dear fellow.
No Barrymore would allow such a
conventional thing to happen to him.'

Béla Bartók (1881–1945)

*Hungarian composer. Musing on his uncompleted work to
the doctor:*

'I am only sad that I have to leave with a
full trunk.'

L. Frank Baum (1856–1919)

American author of The Wonderful Wizard of Oz.
To his wife:

'Now I can cross the shifting sands.'

George Miller Beard (1839–1883)

American neurologist

> 'I should like to record the thoughts of a dying man for the benefit of science, but it is impossible.'

Aubrey Beardsley (1872–1898)

> 'I am imploring you – burn all the indecent poems and drawings.'

Joséphine de Beauharnais (1763–1814)

Wife of Napoleon Bonaparte

> 'Napoleon! Elba! Marie Louise!'

Thomas Becket (*c.* 1117–1170)

Archbishop of Canterbury, murdered in Canterbury Cathedral

> 'For the name of Jesus and the defence of the Church I am willing to die.'

Ludwig van Beethoven (1770–1827)

A case of wine he had ordered from Mainz for his ailing health finally arrived:

'Pity, pity – too late!'

Alexander Graham Bell (1847–1922)

'So little done. So much to do.'

Arnold Bennett (1867–1931)

British journalist and writer. To his mistress:

'Everything's gone wrong, my girl.'

Jeremy Bentham (1748–1832)

'I now feel that I am dying. Our care must be to minimize pain. Do not let the servants come into the room and keep away the youths. It will be distressing to them and they can be of no service.'

Alban Berg (1885–1935)

Austrian composer

'But I have so little time.'

Bernard of Clairvaux (1090–1153)

Abbot and theologian

'May God's will be done.'

Sarah Bernhardt (1844–1923)

French actor

'How slow my death agony is!'

Billy the Kid (1859–1881)

Aka William H. Bonney/Henry McCarty. Notorious outlaw shot by Sheriff Pat Garrett, who ambushed him in a darkened room:

'Who is there?'

Georges Bizet (1838–1875)

French composer

> 'I am in a cold sweat. Is it the sweat of death? How are you going to tell my father?'

William Blake (1757–1827)

To his wife, who asked what songs he was singing:

> 'My beloved, they are not mine, no, they are not mine.'

Anne Boleyn (*c.* 1501–1536)

The day before her execution she was said to have quipped:

> 'I heard say the executioner was very good and I have but a little neck.'

Her final words were:

> 'To Jesus Christ I commend my soul; Lord Jesu receive my soul.'

Napoleon Bonaparte (1769–1821)

'France – army – head of the army – Joséphine.'

John Wilkes Booth (1838–1865)

Assassin of President Abraham Lincoln. To the officer who demanded his surrender:

'Useless! Useless!'

Cesare Borgia (1475–1507)

'I had provided for everything in my life except death, and now, alas! I am to die, though entirely unprepared.'

Dominique Bouhours (1628–1702)

French essayist and grammarian

'I am about to – or am going to – die: either expression is correct.'

Andrew Bradford (1686–1742)

American publisher

> 'Oh Lord, forgive the misprints!'

Tycho Brahe (1546–1601)

Danish astronomer

> 'Let me not seem to have lived in vain.'

Johannes Brahms (1833–1897)

Supping his final glass of wine:

> 'Ah, that tastes nice. Thank you.'

Paulette Brillat-Savarin

Sister of the famous nineteenth-century epicurist Jean Anthelme Brillat-Savarin. Paulette fell ill in the midst of a meal:

> 'Quick! Serve the dessert! I think I am dying.'

Anne Brontë (1820–1849)

To her sister:

'Take courage, Charlotte, take courage!'

Charlotte Brontë (1816–1855)

Speaking to her husband, to whom she had been married for less than a year:

'Oh! I am not going to die, am I? He will not separate us, we have been so happy.'

Emily Brontë (1818–1848)

Having previously refused to see a doctor, Brontë relented too late:

'If you will send for a doctor I will see him now.'

Rupert Brooke (1887–1915)

Dying aboard a hospital ship off the Greek island of Skyros, his last words were in greeting to his final visitor:

'Hello!'

Elizabeth Barrett Browning (1806–1861)

When asked how she was feeling, she replied:

'Beautiful.'

Robert Browning (1812–1889)

On learning that his latest book of poetry Asolando *was selling well:*

'How gratifying.'

Robert Bruce (1554–1631)

Scottish minister and theologian

'Now God be with you, my dear children; I have breakfasted with you, and shall sup with my Lord Jesus Christ.'

George Buchanan (1506–1582)

Scottish historian. After instructing his servant to distribute his property amongst the poor, the servant enquired how burial should be paid for:

> 'It matters little to me; for if I am but once dead they may bury me or not bury me as they please. They may leave my corpse to rot where I die if they wish.'

James Buchanan (1791–1868)

Fifteenth US President

> 'Whatever the result may be, I shall carry to my grave the consciousness that at least I meant well for my country. Oh Lord God Almighty, as thou wilt.'

John Bunyan (1628–1688)

English writer

> 'Take me, for I come to Thee.'

Martin van Buren (1782–1862)

Eighth US President

> 'There is but one reliance …'

Frances Hodgson Burnett (1849–1924)

Author of The Secret Garden

> 'With the best that was in me I have tried to write more happiness into the world.'

Robert Burns (1759–1796)

Referring to the local Dumfries militia, of which he was a member, and of which he held a very low opinion:

> 'Oh, don't let the awkward squad fire over me!'

Richard F. Burton (1821–1890)

Victorian explorer. To his wife:

> 'Oh Puss, chloroform – ether – or I am
> a dead man.'

Lord Byron (1788–1824)

> 'I must sleep now.'

John Calvin (1509–1564)

French theologian

> 'Thou, Lord, bruisest me; but I am
> abundantly satisfied, since it is from
> Thy hand!'

Thomas Carlyle (1795–1881)

Scottish historian

> 'So this is Death. Well!'

Lewis Carroll (1832–1898)

'Take away those pillows – I shall need them no more.'

Edith Cavell (1865–1915)

British nurse shot by the Germans as a spy during the First World War for helping hundreds of Allied soldiers escape occupied Belgium

'I realize that patriotism is not enough. I must have no hatred or bitterness towards anyone.'

Miguel de Cervantes (1547–1616)

Spanish author of Don Quixote

'But adieu, my merry friends all; for I am going to die; and I hope to see you again ere long in the next world as happy as hearts can desire.'

Paul Cézanne (1839–1906)

Delirious, Cézanne said again and again the name of the curator of the Musée Granet which had repeatedly refused his paintings:

'Pontier. Pontier.'

Robert Chambers (1802–1871)

Scottish publisher

'Quite comfortable – quite happy – nothing more!'

Nicolas Chamfort (1741–1794)

French writer. Threatened with imprisonment for his unfettered remarks during the French Revolution, he attempted suicide by shooting himself in the face and stabbing himself with a paper cutter. He survived, horribly injured, for almost a year.

'And so I leave this world, where the heart must either break or turn to lead.'

Charles I (1600–1649)

Executed on 30 January 1649

'My friend, I go from a corruptible crown to an incorruptible, where no disturbance can be.'

Charles II (1630–1685)

These apocryphal last words refer to his mistress the actress, Nell Gwyn:

'Don't let poor Nelly starve!'

His actual last words, after a long illness, were said to be:

'You must pardon me, gentlemen, for being a most unconscionable time a-dying.'

Charles V (1500–1558)

Holy Roman Emperor

'Now, Lord, I go. Ay Jesus!'

Charles IX of France (1550–1574)

*Responsible for the massacre of thousands of Huguenots,
Charles IX died with blood bursting from his own veins:*

> 'What blood! What murders! I know
> not where I am. How will all this end?
> What shall I do? I am lost forever, I
> know it.'

Anton Chekhov (1860–1904)

> 'It is some time since I drank
> champagne.'

Frédéric Chopin (1810–1849)

*Polish pianist and composer. Dying of tuberculosis,
Chopin was said to have uttered:*

> 'The earth is suffocating … Swear to
> make them cut me open, so that I won't
> be buried alive.'

Elizabeth Chudleigh (*c.* 1720–1788)

Georgian socialite and bigamist

> 'I will lie down on the couch; I can sleep, and after that I shall be entirely recovered.'

Samuel Taylor Coleridge (1772–1834)

> 'My mind is quite unclouded, I could even be witty.'

William Collingbourne (*c.* 1435–1484)

Executed for penning the anti-Richard III rhyme 'The Catte, the Ratte, and Lovell our dogge rule all England, under a hogge.' Hung, drawn and quartered, when the executioner put his hand into his body to rip out his heart, Collingbourne said:

> 'Lord Jesus! Yet more trouble?'

Arthur Conan Doyle (1859–1930)

To his wife:

> 'You are wonderful.'

Joseph Conrad (1857–1924)

To his wife:

> 'You, Jess! I'm better this morning! I can always get a rise out of you.'

Calvin Coolidge (1872–1933)

Thirtieth US President. Greeting a carpenter who had come to do some work on his house:

> 'Good morning, Robert.'

Charlotte Corday (1768–1793)

The assassin of Jean-Paul Marat. On seeing the guillotine:

> 'I have a right to be curious, I have never seen one before. It is the toilette of death, but it leads to immortality.'

William Cowper (1731–1800)

English poet

'What can it signify?'

Hart Crane (1899–1932)

American poet who committed suicide by jumping to his death from a cruise ship

'Goodbye everybody.'

Thomas Cranmer (1489–1556)

Archbishop of Canterbury. Cranmer had been forced to sign a recantation of his Protestant faith but was burned at the stake for heresy under the Catholic Mary I. He held out the hand with which he signed the recantation and plunged it into the flames first, saying:

'This unworthy right hand.'

Oliver Cromwell (1599–1658)

'It is not my design to drink or to sleep, but to make what haste I can to be gone.'

William Cullen (1710–1790)

Influential Scottish physician

> 'I wish I had the power of writing,
> for then I would describe to you how
> pleasant a thing it is to die.'

Marie Curie (1867–1934)

To her doctor, who was attempting to give her an injection:

> 'I don't want it. I want to be left alone.'

Georges Cuvier (1769–1832)

French naturalist and zoologist. Unable to swallow, he handed his daughter-in-law a glass of lemonade:

> 'It is delightful to see those whom I love still able to swallow.'

'Jack' Daniel (1850–1911)

American whiskey distiller

> 'One last drink, please'

Georges Jacques Danton (1759–1794)

French Revolutionary leader. Falling foul of his own comrades, he too faced the guillotine as an enemy of the Republic.

'Show my head to the people, it is worth the trouble.'

Charles Darwin (1809–1882)

'I am not in the least afraid to die.'

Daniel Defoe (1660–1731)

'I do not know which is more difficult in a Christian life … to live well or to die well.'

René Descartes (1596–1650)

French philosopher

> 'My soul, thou hast long been held captive; the hour has now come for thee to quit thy prison; to leave the trammels of this body; suffer, then, this separation with joy and courage.'

Charles Dickens (1812–1870)

When Dickens was suddenly taken ill, his sister-in-law suggested that he lie down. Dickens replied:

> 'On the ground.'

Emily Dickinson (1830–1886)

American poet

> 'I must go in, the fog is rising.'

Denis Diderot (1713–1784)

French philosopher. He was reaching for an apricot, and when his wife scolded him, he replied:

> 'But what the devil do you think that that will do to me?'

He died moments later.

Benjamin Disraeli (1804–1881)

> 'I had rather live, but I am not afraid to die.'

John Donne (1572–1631)

English poet

> 'I were miserable, if I might not die.'

Francis Drake (1540–1596)

Drake died of dysentery off the coast of Panama and was buried at sea in a lead-lined coffin to prevent the Spanish from finding his body.

'Help me dress and buckle on my armour, that I might die like a soldier.'

Alexandre Dumas (1802–1870)

To his son Alexandre Dumas fils, referring to his literary works:

'Tell me, Alexandre, on your soul and conscience, do you believe that anything of mine will live?'

Isadora Duncan (1877–1927)

American dancer. Duncan spoke these words as she was driven off in an open-top sports car. Unfortunately her long flowing scarf got caught in the car's axle and broke her neck.

'Farewell, my friends! I go to glory!'

Amelia Earhart (1897–1937)

In a letter to her husband before her last flight she wrote:

> 'Women must try to do things as men have tried. When they fail, their failure must be but a challenge to others.'

George Eastman (1854–1932)

American inventor of the Kodak camera. After a degenerative illness severely affected his mobility he committed suicide; his note read:

> 'To my friends: My work is done. Why wait?'

Thomas Edison (1847–1931)

American inventor

> 'It is very beautiful over there.'

Edward I (1239–1307)

Died while subduing a revolt in Scotland.

> 'Carry my bones before you on your march, for the rebels will not be able to endure the sight of me, alive or dead.'

Edward VII (1841–1910)

After suffering several heart attacks the king was urged to go to bed but refused:

> 'No, I shall not give in; I shall go on; I shall work to the end.'

Later, he was informed that his horse had won at Kempton, to which he replied:

> 'I am very glad.'

George Eliot (1819–1880)

> 'Tell them I have great pain in the left side.'

Elizabeth I (1533–1603)

'All my possessions for one moment of time.'

Ralph Waldo Emerson (1803–1882)

'Goodbye, my friend.'

George Engel (1836–1887)

German anarchist, executed for his part in the Haymarket riot

'Hurrah for anarchy! This is the happiest moment of my life.'

Sergei Esenin (1895–1925)

Russian poet. After a battle with alcoholism and three failed marriages he committed suicide, aged thirty. His suicide note read:

'Goodbye, my friend … There's nothing new in dying now. Though living is no newer.'

William Etty (1787–1849)

English historical painter

'Wonderful, wonderful, this death!'

Douglas Fairbanks (1883–1939)

American actor

'I've never felt better.'

Michael Faraday (1791–1867)

English scientist and inventor. When asked if he had considered what his occupation would be in the next world, he replied:

'I shall be with Christ, and that is enough.'

Paolo Farinato (1524–1606)

Italian painter

'Now I am going.'

It is said as he called out these last words, his wife, who was also ailing, replied, 'I will bear you company, my dear husband', and she too expired.

Franz Ferdinand (1863–1914)

Archduke of Austria. He was assassinated by a Bosnian nationalist, contributing to the outbreak of the First World War.

'It is nothing.'

Johann Gottlieb Fichte (1762–1814)

German philosopher

'Indeed no more medicine; I am well.'

Millard Fillmore (1800–1874)

Thirteenth US President. On being fed some soup:

'The nourishment is palatable.'

Bernard le Bovier de Fontenelle (1657–1757)

French scientist

'I suffer nothing, but feel a sort of difficulty of living longer.'

Charles James Fox (1749–1806)

British Whig statesman. To his wife after she struggled to understand him:

'Trotter will tell you.'

Unfortunately his friend Trotter had not understood either.

Anne Frank (1929–1945)

The last words in her diary, written three days before she was arrested:

'If only there were no other people in the world.'

Benjamin Franklin (1706–1790)

Founding Father of the United States.

'A dying man can do nothing easy.'

Frederick V of Denmark (1723–1766)

'It is a great consolation to me, in my last hour, that I have never wilfully offended anyone, and that there is not a drop of blood on my hands.'

Thomas Gainsborough (1727–1788)

'We are all going to heaven, and Vandyke is of the company.'

Evariste Galois (1811–1832)

French mathematician. Mortally injured after a duel, he said to his brother:

'Don't cry. I need all my courage to die at twenty.'

James A. Garfield (1831–1881)

Twentieth US President. Garfield was assassinated by Charles Julius Guiteau but lingered injured for many months. To his chief of staff David G. Swaim:

'Oh Swaim, there is a pain here. Swaim, can't you stop this? Oh, oh, Swaim!'

Paul Gauguin (1848–1903)

Gauguin's last letter was to his pastor Paul Vernier:

'Would it be troubling you too much to ask you to come to see me? My eyesight seems to be going and I cannot walk. I am very ill.'

George IV (1762–1830)

To his page Sir Wathen Waller:

'Wally, what is this? It is death, my boy.'

George V (1865–1936)

The official last words given out by the palace were:

   'How is the Empire?'

But it is rumoured that his actual last words, in response to his doctor reassuring him that they would soon take him to Bognor to recuperate, were:

   'Bugger Bognor!'

Edward Gibbon (1737–1794)

British author of The History of the Decline and Fall of the Roman Empire

   'All is dark and doubtful.'

W.S. Gilbert (1836–1911)

British librettist. While he was giving two children a swimming lesson in a lake, one slipped and Gilbert dived in to help, saying:

   'Put your hands on my shoulders and don't struggle.'

He then suffered a heart attack and died.

Charlotte Perkins Gilman (1860–1935)

American feminist and writer. After being diagnosed with incurable cancer she committed suicide, writing:

> 'It is the simplest of human rights to choose a quick and easy death in place of a slow and horrible one.'

Johann Wolfgang von Goethe (1749–1832)

German writer and poet

> 'More light! More light!'

Katharina Elisabeth von Goethe (1731–1808)

Mother of the celebrated German writer Johann von Goethe. A prolific letter-writer, her final missive replied to an invitation from friends who did not know of her illness:

> 'I must ask to be excused, as I have to die.'

Oliver Goldsmith (1728–1774)

Anglo-Irish novelist. To his doctor, who asked if his mind was at ease:

> 'No, it is not!'

Ulysses S. Grant (1822–1885)

Eighteenth US President.

> 'Water.'

Joseph Henry Green (1791–1863)

English surgeon. Green was feeling for his own pulse and said:

> 'Stopped.'

Lady Jane Grey (1537–1554)

Queen for just nine days, she was beheaded for treason aged seventeen.

> 'Lord, into Thy hands I commend my spirit.'

Edvard Grieg (1843–1907)

Norwegian composer.

> 'Well, if it must be so.'

Nathan Hale (1755–1776)

Soldier in the Continental Army during the American Revolutionary Wars, executed by the British as a spy.

> 'I only regret that I have but one life to give to my country!'

Warren Harding (1865–1923)

Twenty-ninth US President. Listening as his wife read him flattering newspaper reports, he said:

> 'That's good. Go on. Read some more.'

Joel Chandler Harris (1848–1908)

American writer and folklorist. When asked how he felt, he replied:

> 'I am about the extent of a tenth of a gnat's eyebrow better.'

Benjamin Harrison (1833–1901)

Twenty-third US President

'Are the doctors here?'

William Henry Harrison (1773–1841)

Ninth US President. To his vice president, John Tyler:

'Sir, I wish you to understand the true principles of government. I wish them carried out. I ask nothing more.'

Franz Joseph Haydn (1732–1809)

'Cheer up children, I'm all right.'

Rutherford Hayes (1822–1893)

Nineteenth US President. Speaking about his beloved wife, Lucy:

'I know that I am going where Lucy is.'

William Hazlitt (1778–1830)

English essayist

> 'I have led a happy life.'

Heinrich Heine (1797–1856)

German poet

> 'God will pardon me, that's his line of work.'

Héloïse (1101–1164)

Scholar, nun and lover of Peter Abelard

> 'In death at last let me rest with Abelard.'

O. Henry (1862–1910)

> 'Turn up the lights, I don't want to go home in the dark.'

Henry VIII (1491–1547)

When asked if he would like to consult with a learned man, Henry replied:

> 'If I had any, it should be Dr Cranmer, but I will first take a little sleep, and then, as I feel myself, I will advise upon the matter.'

Thomas Hobbes (1588–1679)

English philosopher

> 'I am about to take my last voyage, a great leap in the dark.'

Ludwig Holty (1748–1776)

German poet

> 'I am very ill. Send for Zimmerman. In fact, I think I'll die today.'

Gerard Manley Hopkins (1844–1889)

British poet and Jesuit priest

> 'I am so happy, I am so happy. I loved my life.'

Harry Houdini (1874–1926)

> 'I'm tired of fighting, Dash. I guess this thing is going to get me.'

A.E. Housman (1859–1936)

British poet and classical scholar. After being told a joke by his doctor:

> 'That is indeed very good. I shall have to repeat that on the Golden Floor!'

Robert E. Howard (1906–1936)

American pulp writer who committed suicide. The note found on his typewriter quoted a poem by Viola Garvin:

> 'All fled, all done, so lift me on the pyre; The feast is over and the lamps expire.'

Victor Hugo (1802–1885)

French writer

'I see the black light.'

Alexander von Humboldt (1769–1859)

German explorer

'How grand the sunlight! It seems to beckon earth to heaven.'

Henrik Ibsen (1828–1906)

Norwegian playwright. In response to a nurse who said he seemed a little better he replied:

'On the contrary!'

Washington Irving (1783–1859)

American author and essayist

'Well, I must arrange my pillows for another night. When will this end?'

Andrew Jackson (1767–1845)

Seventh US President

> 'I hope to meet you all in Heaven. Be good children, all of you, and strive to be ready when the change comes.'

Thomas 'Stonewall' Jackson (1824–1863)

Confederate general. Jackson was accidentally shot by his own soldiers during a night-time gun battle. Mortally wounded, he died in delirium.

> 'Let us go over the river, and sit under the refreshing shadow of the trees.'

Henry James (1843–1916)

American writer

> 'Tell the boys to follow, to be faithful, to take me seriously.'

James II (1633–1701)

Died in exile in France after being ousted by William III and Mary II (his daughter) in the Glorious Revolution of 1688

'Grateful – in peace!'

James V of Scotland (1512–42)

Referring to the Scottish crown and the imminent accession of his daughter, Mary:

'It came with a lass, and it will go with a lass.'

Thomas Jefferson (1743–1826)

Third US President. He died on 4 July as the nation was celebrating the fiftieth anniversary of the Declaration of Independence, just hours before his fellow signatory John Adams.

'Is it the fourth?'

Dr Samuel Johnson (1709–1784)

When told he would not recover:

> 'Then I will take no more physic, not even my opiates; for I have prayed that I may render up my soul to God unclouded.'

His very last words were:

> 'God bless you, my dear.'

Joseph II (1741–1790)

Holy Roman Emperor

> 'Let my epitaph be, Here lies Joseph, who was unsuccessful in all his undertakings.'

James Joyce (1862–1941)

> 'Does nobody understand?'

Franz Kafka (1883–1924)

Writer. Kafka died of tuberculosis and starvation as he could no longer swallow food. In his desperate state he pleaded with the doctor:

'Kill me, or you are a murderer!'

John Keats (1795–1821)

British poet who died from tuberculosis

'Severn, lift me up – I am dying – I shall die easy; don't be frightened – be firm and thank God it has come.'

Ned Kelly (1855–1880)

Australian outlaw. On the gallows:

'Such is life!'

Rudyard Kipling (1865–1936)

To his doctor:

'Something has come adrift inside.'

Thomas Fantet de Lagny (1660–1734)

French mathematician. He was lying so still that it was thought he might already be dead, but when his friend asked what the square of twelve was, de Lagny instantly replied:

'144.'

Pierre-Simon de Laplace (1749–1827)

French mathematician and astronomer

'What we know is not much. What we don't know is enormous.'

D.H. Lawrence (1885–1930)

'I think it is time for morphine.'

Edward Lear (1812–1888)

To his servant:

> 'I cannot find words sufficient to thank my good friends for the good they have always done me. I did not answer their letters because I could not write, as no sooner did I take my pen in my hand than I felt as if I were dying.'

Vladimir Ilych Lenin (1870–1924)

To his dog, who had brought him a dead bird:

> 'Good dog.'

Vachel Lindsay (1879–1931)

American poet who committed suicide. His note read:

> 'They tried to get me – I got them first!'

George Lippard (1822–1854)

American author and social activist. To his doctor:

> 'Is this death?'

Henry Wadsworth Longfellow (1807–1882)

When his sister arrived to visit, he said:

> 'Now I know that I must be very ill, since you have been sent for.'

Louis the Pious (778–840)

King of the Franks. When he heard that his son was revolting against him, he was reported to have quipped:

> 'I pardon him, but let him know that it is on his account that I am dying.'

Louis XIV (1638–1715)

> 'Why weep you? Did you think I should live forever?'

Then after a pause:

> 'I thought dying had been harder.'

Louis XVI (1754–1793)

Guillotined during the French Revolution

> 'I die innocent of all the crimes laid to my charge; I pardon those who have occasioned my death; and I pray to God that the blood you are going to shed may never be visited on France.'

Louis XVIII (1755–1824)

Trying to rise from his bed:

> 'A king should die standing.'

Martin Luther (1483–1546)

Leader of the Protestant Reformation. He was asked if he stood by his doctrines of scripture and answered:

> 'Yes.'

Thomas Babington Macaulay (1800–1859)

British politician and writer

'I shall retire early; I am very tired.'

Niccolò Machiavelli (1469–1527)

Italian politician and writer

'I desire to go to hell, and not to heaven. In the former place I shall enjoy the company of popes, kings, and princes, while in the latter are only beggars, monks, hermits, and apostles.'

James Mackintosh (1765–1832)

Scottish politician. When asked how he felt, he replied:

'Happy!'

James Madison (1751–1836)

Fourth US President

'I always talk better lying down.'

Gustav Mahler (1860–1911)

Austrian composer

'Mozart! Mozart!'

Jean-Paul Marat (1743–1793)

French Revolutionary leader assassinated in his bath by Charlotte Corday. To his wife:

'Help me, my dear friend!'

Guglielmo Marconi (1874–1937)

Italian inventor

'I'm feeling awfully ill.'

Marie Antoinette (1755–1793)

Wife of Louis XVI, she was guillotined on 16 October 1793. After tripping on the foot of the executioner:

> 'Monsieur, I beg your pardon. I did not do it on purpose.'

Karl Marx (1818–1883)

In response to his housekeeper, who asked if he had any final message to pass on:

> 'Go on, get out! Last words are for fools who haven't said enough.'

Mary I (1516–1558)

Commonly called 'Bloody Mary'

> 'After I am dead, you will find Calais written upon my heart.'

Mary II (1662–1694)

Queen of England and wife of William III. Archbishop Tillotson was reading a prayer to her on her deathbed and was overcome with emotion:

'My Lord, why do you not go on? I am not afraid to die.'

Mary, Queen of Scots (1542–1587)

Executed for plotting to overthrow Elizabeth I

'O Lord, into Thy hands I commend my spirit.'

Cotton Mather (1663–1728)

New England Puritan minister, pamphleteer and supporter of the Salem witch trials

'I am going where all tears will be wiped from my eyes.'

Jules Mazarin (1602–1661)

Cardinal and First Minister of France under Louis XIV

'O, my poor soul, what is to become of thee? Whither wilt thou go?'

William McKinley (1843–1901)

Twenty-fifth US President. After an assassination attempt during which he was shot twice in the stomach, McKinley lingered for days before succumbing to gangrene.

'Goodbye, goodbye to all. It is God's way. His will be done – not ours.'

Richard B. Mellon (1858–1933)

American banker. Mellon whispered to his brother Andrew, with whom he had been playing tag for over seventy years:

'Last tag.'

Andrew remained 'it' for another four years until he too died and the game could recommence on the other side.

Herman Melville (1819–1891)

American novelist. Referring to a character in his latest book:

'God Bless Captain Vere!'

Felix Mendelssohn (1809–1847)

When asked how he felt:

'Weary, very weary.'

Albert Abraham Michelson (1852–1931)

Nobel Prize-winning American physicist. Right up to his death he was still carrying out experiments; his final log entry reads:

'The following is a report on the measurement of the velocity of light made at the Irvine Ranch, near Santa Ana, California, during the period of September 1929 to ...'

Glenn Miller (1904–1944)

American Big Band musician. As he boarded a plane, he exclaimed:

'Where the hell are the parachutes?'

The plane went missing over the English Channel.

Richard Monckton Milnes (1809–1885)

English poet

'My exit is the result of too many entrees.'

Wilson Mizner (1876–1933)

American playwright. A priest said to him, 'I'm sure you want to talk to me.' Mizner replied:

'Why should I talk to you? I've just been talking to your boss.'

Molière (1622–1673)

Molière collapsed on stage while performing Le Malade Imaginaire *(The Imaginary Invalid) and was taken home to die:*

> 'Don't be frightened, you've seen me
> bring up more [blood] than that.
> However, go and tell my wife to
> come up.'

James Monroe (1758–1831)

Fifth US President. Speaking of his best friend, the fourth US President James Madison:

> 'I regret that I should leave this world
> without again beholding him.'

Lady Mary Wortley Montagu (1689–1762)

Prolific letter-writer and essayist

> 'It has all been most interesting.'

Simon de Montfort (1208–1265)

Earl of Leicester, leader of rebellion against Henry III, killed at the Battle of Evesham. On hearing that his son Henry had been killed, he said, 'Then it is time for us to die.' His final words as he was slain were:

'Thank God.'

Thomas More (1478–1535)

More was beheaded for treason for refusing to recognize the marriage of Henry VIII and Anne Boleyn. His last words were addressed to the executioner:

'Stay, friend, till I put aside my beard, for that never committed treason.'

William Morris (1834–1896)

'I have enjoyed my life – few more so.'

Wolfgang Amadeus Mozart (1756–1791)

'I have the flavour of death on my tongue. I taste death.'

Later he conversed with Süssmayer over the Requiem and was heard to say:

'Did I not say that I was writing the Requiem for myself?'

Adam Naruszewicz (1733–1796)

Polish bishop and historian. Referring to his life's work, a history of Poland:

'Must I leave it unfinished?'

Lord Horatio Nelson (1758–1805)

A number of final words were recorded after Nelson was hit by a sniper and lay below deck dying, including: 'Take care of poor Lady Hamilton – Kiss me Hardy.' 'God bless you Hardy'. The final final words were:

'Thank God, I have done my duty.'

Isaac Newton (1643–1727)

Newton wrote in his last letter:

> 'I do not know what I may appear
> to the world, but to myself I seem to
> have been only like a boy playing on
> the sea-shore, and diverting himself
> in now and then finding a smoother
> pebble or a prettier shell than ordinary,
> while the great ocean of truth lies all
> undiscovered before me.'

Florence Nightingale (1820–1910)

On receiving the Order of Merit on her deathbed:

> 'Too kind – too kind.'

Nostradamus (1503–1566)

> 'You will not see me alive at sunrise.'

Lawrence Oates (1880–1912)

Antarctic explorer, part of Robert Falcon Scott's team, who sacrificed himself in the vain effort to save his comrades

> 'I am just going outside and may be some time.'

Titus Oates (1649–1705)

Fabricator of the 'Popish Plot' to kill King Charles II

> 'It is all the same in the end.'

Wilfred Owen (1893–1918)

First World War poet. In his last letter to his mother, written four days before he was killed in action:

> 'There is no danger down here, or if any, it will be well over before you read these lines.'

Thomas Paine (1737–1809)

British-American political activist and revolutionary

> 'I would give worlds, if I had them, that the "Age of Reason" had never been published. Oh, God, save me; for I am at the edge of hell alone …'

John Palmer (1742–1798)

Celebrated British actor who died on stage. His last words were a line in the play, The Stranger:

> 'There is another and a better world.'

Viscount Palmerston (1784–1865)

Two-times UK prime minister. His apocryphal last words were said to be:

> 'Die, my dear doctor? That's the last thing I shall do.'

A famous workaholic, his actual last words were:

> 'That's Article ninety-eight; now go on to the next.'

Blaise Pascal (1623–1662)

French mathematician and philosopher

'May God never abandon me!'

Louis Pasteur (1822–1895)

French chemist. Responding when he was offered a glass of milk:

'I cannot.'

Anna Pavlova (1881–1931)

Celebrated ballerina

'Get my swan costume ready.'

Spencer Perceval (1762–1812)

British prime minister assassinated in the lobby of the House of Commons by John Bellingham

'Oh my God!'

William Pitt, the Younger (1759–1806)

There is some dispute over whether Pitt's final words were:

'Oh my country, how I leave thee!'

or

'Oh my country! How I love thee!'

Edgar Allan Poe (1809–1849)

Poe was found wandering, delirious, on the streets of Baltimore, dressed in clothes which were not his own. His last words were:

'Lord help my soul!'

James K. Polk (1795–1849)

Eleventh US President. To his wife:

'I love you Sarah. For all eternity, I love you.'

Marco Polo (1254–1324)

'I have not told half of what I saw.'

Alexander Pope (1688–1744)

British poet

> 'I am dying, sir, of a hundred good symptoms.'

Joseph Priestley (1733–1804)

British scientist and philosopher

> 'I am going to sleep like you, but we shall all awake together, and I trust to everlasting happiness.'

François Rabelais (*c.* 1494–1553)

French writer

> 'Let down the curtain, the farce is over.'

Some say his last words were:

> 'I am going to the great perhaps.'

Walter Raleigh (*c.* 1552–1618)

About to be executed for treason, Raleigh asked to examine the axe and quipped:

'This is a sharp medicine, but a sure remedy for all evils!'

He was then said to have addressed the hesitating executioner:

'Why dost thou not strike? Strike!'

Jean-Philippe Rameau (1683–1764)

French composer. To the priest singing at his bedside:

'What the devil do you mean to sing to me, priest? You are out of tune.'

Raphael (1483–1520)

Renaissance artist

'Happy.'

Pierre-Auguste Renoir (1841–1919)

French Impressionist painter. Referring to his skills as an artist:

'I think I'm beginning to understand something about it.'

Joshua Reynolds (1723–1792)

British portrait painter

'I know that all things on earth must have an end, and now I am come to mine.'

Cecil Rhodes (1853–1902)

British imperialist and politician

'So much to do; so little done. Goodbye. God bless you.'

Rainer Maria Rilke (1875–1926)

Austrian poet

> 'I don't want the doctor's death. I want to have my own freedom.'

Theodore Roosevelt (1858–1919)

Twenty-sixth US President

> 'Please put out the light.'

Christina Rossetti (1830–1894)

British poet

> 'I love everybody. If ever I had an enemy I should hope to meet and welcome that enemy in heaven.'

Dante Gabriel Rossetti (1828–82)

Pre-Raphaelite writer and painter

> 'I think I shall die tonight.'

Jean Jacques Rousseau (1712–1778)

French philosopher and writer

> 'Throw up the window that I may see once more the magnificent scene of nature.'

Saki (1870–1916)

Pen name of British writer H.H. Munro. He was killed by a sniper's bullet during the First World War just after saying:

> 'Put that bloody cigarette out.'

Maurice de Saxe (1696–1750)

Marshal of France

> 'The dream has been short, but it has been beautiful.'

Egon Schiele (1890–1918)

Austrian artist who died of Spanish flu in the final days of the First World War

'The war is over and I must go.'

Friedrich Schiller (1759–1805)

German dramatist and poet

'Many things are growing plain and clear to me.'

Franz Schubert (1797–1828)

Austrian composer

'Here, here is my end.'

Robert Falcon Scott (1868–1912)

Scott and his comrades perished during their ill-fated expedition to be first to reach the South Pole. Scott's last journal entry concluded:

'For God's sake look after our people.'

Thomas Scott (1535–1594)

English politician

> 'Until this moment, I thought there was neither God nor Hell ... Now I know and feel that there are both, and I am doomed to perdition by the just judgment of the Almighty ...'

Walter Scott (1771–1832)

To his assembled family:

> 'God bless you all! I feel as if I were to be myself again.'

John Sedgwick (1813–1864)

Union army general killed in battle during the US Civil War

> 'They couldn't hit an elephant at this distance!'

William Henry Seward (1801–1872)

American politician. When asked if he had any final words he replied:

> 'Nothing, only love one another.'

Ernest Shackleton (1874–1922)

To his doctor:

> 'You are always wanting me to give up something. What do you want me to give up now?'

Adam Smith (1723–1790)

Smith was in the habit of dining with a group of friends on a Sunday night:

> 'I believe we must adjourn this meeting to some other place.'

Bessie Smith (1894–1937)

American blues singer

> 'I'm going, but I'm going in the name of the Lord.'

Tobias Smollett (1721–1771)

Scottish writer

> 'All is well, my dear.'

Socrates (*c.* 470–399 BC)

Found guilty of impiety by the state and forced to commit suicide by drinking hemlock:

> 'Crito, we owe a cock to Asclepius. Do pay it. Don't forget.'

Robert Louis Stevenson (1850–1894)

He seemed to feel a sudden pain in his head; he clasped his forehead and cried:

> 'What is that?'

Lytton Strachey (1880–1932)

British writer and critic

'If this is dying, I don't think much of it.'

Johann Strauss II (1825–1889)

On being told to go to sleep, he replied:

'I will, whatever happens.'

August Strindberg (1849–1912)

Swedish playwright. He died clutching a Bible, saying:

'It is atoned for.'

Zachary Taylor (1784–1850)

Twelfth US President

'I am about to die. I expect the summons very soon. I have tried to discharge all my duties faithfully. I regret nothing, but I am sorry that I am about to leave my friends.'

Alfred, Lord Tennyson (1809–1892)

'I have opened it.'

Henry David Thoreau (1817–1862)

American naturalist and writer. In his delirium:

'Moose … Indian…'

Leo Tolstoy (1828–1910)

'I love many things, I love all people …'

Leon Trotsky (1879–1940)

On his way to hospital after he had been attacked with an ice axe:

'I think Stalin has finished the job he has started.'

Harriet Tubman (1822–1913)

American abolitionist. As her family gathered around her deathbed, she led them all in song; her final words were:

'Swing low, sweet chariot.'

J.M.W. Turner (1775–1851)

'The sun is God.'

Mark Twain (1835–1910)

A note found by Twain's deathbed read: 'Death, the only immortal, who treats us alike, whose peace and refuge are for all. The soiled and the pure, the rich and the poor, the loved and the unloved.' His final spoken words were to his daughter, Clara:

'Goodbye, if we meet …'

John Tyler (1790–1862)

Tenth US President. On his deathbed he said, 'Doctor, I am going.' The doctor replied 'I hope not, sir.' Tyler's final words were:

'Perhaps it is best.'

William Tyndale (1484–1536)

English scholar and translator of the Bible into English who was executed for heresy

> 'Lord, open the eyes of the King of England!'

Rudolph Valentino (1895–1926)

> 'Don't pull down the blinds. I feel fine. I want the sunlight to greet me!'

Jules Verne (1828–1905)

French writer. To his family:

> 'Good, you're all there. Now I can die.'

Vespasian (AD 9–79)

Roman emperor

> 'An Emperor ought to die standing.'

Queen Victoria (1819–1901)

To her son, Edward, Prince of Wales:

'Bertie.'

Pancho Villa (1878–1923)

Mexican revolutionary leader

'Don't let it end like this. Tell them I said something.'

Leonardo da Vinci (1452–1519)

'I have offended God and mankind because my work did not reach the quality it should have.'

Voltaire (1694–1778)

A famous critic of the Catholic Church, Voltaire's last words were directed at someone praying at his bedside:

> 'For the love of God, don't mention that Man – allow me to die in peace!'

Others have it that when asked to renounce Satan, Voltaire replied:

> 'Now, now, my good man, this is not time to be making enemies.'

Richard Wagner (1813–1883)

German composer. After Wagner suffered a heart attack his wife helped him to a chair and his watch fell from his pocket; he exclaimed:

> 'Oh, my watch!'

Henry Ward Beecher (1813–1887)

American abolitionist and social reformer

> 'Now comes the mystery.'

Charles Dudley Warner (1829–1900)

American essayist and novelist

> 'I am not well, and should like to lie
> down – will you call me in ten minutes?
> Thank you. You are very kind – in ten
> minutes – remember!'

George Washington (1732–99)

First US President

> 'Doctor, I am dying, and have been
> dying for a long time; but I am not
> afraid to die.'

Daniel Webster (1782–1852)

American statesman

> 'I still live!'

Duke of Wellington (1769–1852)

To his valet:

> 'Do you know where the apothecary lives? Then send and let him know that I should like to see him. I don't feel quite well and I will lie still till he comes.'

William Wilberforce (1759–1833)

British politician, philanthropist and abolitionist. His son, Henry, wishing to comfort his dying father, said, 'You have your feet on the Rock.' Wilberforce answered:

> 'I do not venture to speak so positively, but I hope I have.'

Oscar Wilde (1854–1900)

> 'My wallpaper and I are fighting a duel to the death. One or other of us has got to go.'

William III (of Orange) (1650–1702)

The king was mortally injured after his horse tripped on a molehill. To his doctors:

> 'I know that you have done all that skill and learning could do for me: but the case is beyond your art; and I submit.'

William the Silent, Prince of Orange (1533–1584)

Founder of the Dutch Republic. When asked if he commended his soul to Jesus Christ, he replied:

> 'I do.'

Woodrow Wilson (1856–1924)

Twenty-eighth US President

> 'I am a broken piece of machinery. When the machine is broken … I am ready.'

Thomas Wolfe (1900–1938)

American novelist. As he was dying in hospital he wrote a final letter to his friend, Maxwell Perkins:

> 'I've made a long voyage and been to a strange country, and I've seen the dark men very close; and I don't think I was too much afraid of him, but so much of mortality still clings to me – I wanted most desperately to live and still do ...'

Mary Wollstonecraft (1759–1797)

British feminist writer. Dying of complications after childbirth, she spoke to her husband who was trying to prepare her for death:

> 'I know what you are thinking of, but I have nothing to communicate on the subject of religion.'

Virginia Woolf (1882–1941)

In a suicide note to her husband:

> 'I have a feeling I shall go mad. I cannot go on any longer in these terrible times. I hear voices and cannot concentrate on my work. I have fought against it but cannot fight any longer. I owe my happiness to you but cannot go on and spoil your life.'

William Wordsworth (1770–1850)

His wife, knowing he was dying, told him he was going to their daughter, Dora, in heaven. Many hours later as his niece drew the curtain, he whispered:

> 'God bless you! Is that you, Dora?'

Joseph Wright (1855–1930)

English linguist and editor of the English Dialect Dictionary. *His final word was the very apt:*

> 'Dictionary.'

Brigham Young (1801–1877)

Mormon leader and founder of Utah

'I feel better.'

Florenz Ziegfeld (1867–1932)

American impresario and showman. In his delirium:

'Curtain! Fast music! Light! Ready for the last finale! Great! The show looks good, the show looks good!'

Emile Zola (1840–1902)

French writer. To his wife as they unwittingly struggled with carbon monoxide poisoning:

'I feel sick. My head is splitting. No, don't you see the dog is sick too? We are both ill. It must be something we have eaten. It will pass away. Let's not bother them.'

Ulrich Zwingli (1484–1531)

Leader of the Reformation in Switzerland who died in battle:

> 'What does it matter? They may kill the body, but they cannot kill the soul.'

Sources

Bega, *Last Words of Famous Men* (London: Williams & Norgate, 1930).

Birrell, Francis and F.L. Lucas, *The Art of Dying* (London: Hogarth Press, 1930).

Brandreth, Gyles, *Famous Last Words and Tombstone Humour* (New York: Sterling, 1989).

Breverton, Terry, *Immortal Last Words* (London: Quercus, 2010).

Le Comte, Edward, *Dictionary of Last Words* (New York: Philosophical Library, 1955).

Conrad, Barnaby, *Famous Last Words* (New York: Doubleday, 1961).

Green, Jonathan, *Famous Last Words* (London: Kyle Cathie, 2002).

Hom, Susan K., *RIP: Here Lie the Last Words, Morbid Musings, Epitaphs and Fond Farewells of the Famous and Not-so-famous* (New York: Sterling, 2007).

J.M.H., *Last Words of 500 Remarkable Persons* (London: Partridge and Co., 1876).

Marvin, Frederic Rowland, *The Last Words of Distinguished Men and Women (Real and Traditional)* (New York: Revell, 1901).

O'Kill, Brian, *Exit Lines* (London: Longman, 1986).

Ruffin, C. Bernard, *Last Words: A Dictionary of Deathbed Quotations* (New York: Macfarland, 1995).

Thorp, Peter and Reggie Sharp, *The Paragon Book of Famous Last Words* (London: Paragon, 2000).